was i *feeling* too much?

was i *feeling* too much?

luis gabriel

just words trying to mean something to someone.

was i *feeling* too much?

with time he noticed she was a little more fragile

than she had let on,

a little less composed-

completely ruined by a newfound sadness.

today felt like the first day of spring. the air felt clean, the sky was blue and my limbs were all attached. yesterday, all my skeletons and the shells of myself withered off and left only disproportioned pieces. by morning i had lost my head, i had left my arms at noon and was left without the skin on my feet by nightfall. by midnight i was a beating membrane wrapped in two cages. i was broken and yet this morning when i woke, i was new and although the sky was gray yesterday- today it is blue.

was i *feeling* too much?

i realized the words from my mouth

meant nothing to you,

even after i had moved them onto paper.

luis gabriel

you're saying i'm not who i used to be,

maybe you got used to me,

a version of me you hadn't hurt.

was i *feeling* too much?

you taught me that even in holding your hand,

i could still feel lonely.

he said he loved me but-

he was always looking for love in the wrong places,

it tasted,

like somebody else,

everybody else,

anybody else,

one chases,

the thing that makes you not just anyone else.

was i *feeling* too much?

it's the way they used to love us...

that's what we miss.

12:59

sometimes i think we all wish that we

felt a little more important,

a little less transparent,

that something or someone would be more

observant,

to take notice,

to see us for what we really are and who we

struggle to be.

1:00

was i *feeling* too much?

she told everyone "i want to fall in love but i don't

feel safe anywhere".

luis gabriel

that night we were both in love with strangers,

you were loving someone else and i was loving you.

was i *feeling* too much?

she was always wondering if she was

the one messing things up,

bringing up things from the past that

she hadn't learned to let go of.

he gave up when "i love yous"

began to feel like "i owe yous".

was i *feeling* too much?

we had everything we wanted,

we were the only things missing.

he realized he couldn't ask for the love that had

never been there before.

was i *feeling* too much?

he had asked her " why'd you stop loving me?"

she told him that "loving you won't fix everything".

it's like you don't know me anymore,

you keep talking to me like it's the old me-

the person you knew before.

was i *feeling* too much?

she said she only loves her when it's 3 am because

that's when she feels lonely.

when the silence is so loud in her empty home.

luis gabriel

we're so mad that we grew up to be so sad.

was i *feeling* too much?

"i love you" felt forever away.

when she saw that his actions no longer

matched his whispered promises,

she tore the pages out of the unfinished

book and finished it.

was i *feeling* too much?

she just needed to know if he'd stay.

this time her chest hurt a little,

like someone had set a paperweight

on it,

she couldn't explain it,

didn't try to entertain it,

she closed her eyes and tried to let the sun wash the

feeling away.

she didn't mean to say-

that it felt like his words weren't

enough.

because in reality,

they meant the world.

was i *feeling* too much?

she felt the cold inside her bones,

maybe this time she would make it hers

and call it home.

his face,

the cold cruel chill,

that could never fill,

the little spaces in her chest or the cavities in her

mind,

even found it hard to find,

any recollection of anything

resembling the magic she had once

felt left behind.

was i *feeling* too much?

i'm scared to think that you were just lonely,

that i happened to be there when you

needed a distraction,

when all you needed was someone to

fill up your empty spaces,

the heartbroken places,

i could never set foot in.

luis gabriel

maybe it was the "caution hot !!"

coffee in his hands,

the warm sun trailing light touches

down his neck,

the soft song of traffic around him,

that he started to feel truly at peace.

it was the type of peace he'd

remember tomorrow if things

crumbled and didn't go as planned.

was i *feeling* too much?

she had a strength that fueled solar systems and a

love that decorated galaxies.

he suddenly felt so seen in places he felt he was the

most invisible,

not the crowded spaces,

just the places he wore his soul out on

his sleeves.

was i *feeling* too much?

he said " he only likes it when i'm sad,

when i'm easy to manipulate,

when it's easily convenient to forget

to compensate-

for the shit, he keeps pulling."

when he asked her if the poems she'd written

yesterday were about him,

she told him no.

even though,

they both knew the explanations and sloppy

metaphors were linked to him,

words she had, with shaky hands, typed out on her

keypad, he told her they made him sad.

made him feel bad,

like he was always doing something wrong,

and when he asked her what little things

did he ever do right, she never had an answer.

they were never supposed to be or have the answer,

they were never supposed to be a part of the same

equation, part of the same sentence, share the

same timed memories.

was i *feeling* too much?

he could see slivers of golden heaven pooling in her

eyes.

luis gabriel

she wasn't looking for perfect,

she was just looking for someone she

could hold and feel like she

was finally home.

was i *feeling* too much?

forgetting about the past ones,

the old times,

i finally felt like the muse on my mind

was all mine,

no half promises,

no half met feelings,

just all the right cards in the right hands,

cards that i wouldn't be scared of dealing.

maybe all the wrong words were

being said.

or maybe they were the right words.

only the emotions behind them were all dead.

was i *feeling* too much?

she should have saved the words she'd

said to him,

for someone who would have had the

guts to say them back.

luis gabriel

she was always lonely,

even the walls in her home that had

seen so much,

no longer kept the memory of all that had

happened.

was i *feeling* too much?

his love had isolated itself,

it wouldn't come out until it finally felt

safe.

she wondered when his *i miss yous*

would stop being enough.

was i *feeling* too much?

he didn't have enough poems,

enough words,

enough thoughts to capture his lovers essence,

it was magic and it could not be

contained.

take her back to the night you met,

tell her all the pretty words,

not the ones you say now that cause her

to isolate and hurt,

take her back to the night you met,

when you would have brought down the

stars for her,

not the nights that end in hazy

argumentative blurs,

take her back to the night you met,

when heaven was on earth and hell was

the space between laced fingers.

was i *feeling* too much?

when i got mad i pushed him away,

he was mad that i didn't let him stay,

he said that he couldn't handle the

smoke but he always set me on fire,

told me that i cried too much but

never took credit for being a liar.

what bothered her was that she'd

never have all the love she had given

him, back. it would linger with him

until he no longer held an audience in

the world. she would always be giving

someone something that was broken and

someone something more broken to the

next and the next. an unending cycle

of brokenness she would have never

imagined being someone else's gold mine.

was i *feeling* too much?

she loved him more than she had ever

loved herself,

and done more for him than she would have ever

imagined doing for herself.

luis gabriel

i used to close my eyes and tell

everyone i was over you,

but every night when the waves of

sleep washed over me i was under you,

pretending my head was in the clouds

when it was lost in you.

now i'm over you,

big blue sky over small city- over you.

music caught in the wind of open

windows of my car that should

remind me of you- but it

doesn't, over you.

we made a mess out of love,

let's hope the definition we gave it

doesn't ruin it for the people after you...

for the people after me.

i've been dealing with nightmares,

there aren't any demons under my bed,

just the ghosts of the things you said and never

meant.

was i *feeling* too much?

my poems say i escaped you,

and for me,

that will always be enough.

luis gabriel

in a city so small i've managed to miss you at every

corner.

was i *feeling* too much?

she felt replaceable,

cried herself to sleep because she felt

erase-able.

maybe if she hugged herself tighter she

wouldn't disappear.

miles away and he could still make her smile.

was i *feeling* too much?

you made me feel so small,

and so sad,

that it makes me mad,

to think that i ever felt anything at all.

luis gabriel

the things we said when we were

angry

drove us six feet apart

but i'm feeling like i'm six feet

under.

was i *feeling* too much?

you don't look at me the same way,

the way you did before i hurt you.

luis gabriel

you are divine.

was i *feeling* too much?

the worst parts of you are the ones

i find myself daydreaming about.

the best parts of you are the ones that could make eternity

seem too short.

it was never about being seen,

everybody saw her,

but so little understood her.

was i *feeling* too much?

a long time ago,

i imagined being home for you,

but i had a feeling that i'd still feel empty.

just four walls with windows for eyes.

maybe his words would mean

different things tomorrow,

maybe he wouldn't mean them all.

maybe he should have strapped

himself in before the fall.

was i *feeling* too much?

you stopped feeling like home,

when i started to feel like a stranger.

when the insecurities talked,

we sat them down,

and tore them open,

scared glances,

our first romances-

defined what we had.

when the insecurities talked,

we shared small glances,

slow dances,

hid them under the bed we made,

should have known that nothing

grows away from the sun under the

shade.

maybe if we had been honest,

cleaned the whole room,

nothing hidden in the closet-

things would have been okay.

was i *feeling* too much?

he felt familiar,

like he had known him for a lifetime.

the stars hung in the sky before you

but you make them shine so much

brighter.

was i *feeling* too much?

we were supposed to save each

other from our darkest days,

but instead, we made them.

maybe our words were everything

they were trying to be,

nothing hiding behind them,

no pretending,

or sending-

mixed messages.

when you pulled me down with you,

i agreed to sink,

to drift beneath the soft blue,

because that's what love was right?

following you into the dark,

and holding your hand when you choked

on the stinging currents, the chaotic

blues.

luis gabriel

i remember when i spent the night in

your arms,

my head resting so close to the beating *thump*

thump of your heart.

was i *feeling* too much?

home had become a feeling not a place.

she looked up at him,

into him,

always wondering if home was a feeling

or a place for him,

if it was the sadness behind her eyes or

the gap between her thighs,

which one was home?

was i *feeling* too much?

maybe the memories that i hold onto

are the ones you never cared about.

luis gabriel

would you stand in the rain with me?

under the gray sky of a lonely beach

or in the middle of the night when i'm

feeling blue.

old loves damaged us so badly,

we're so scared to be human,

too scared to ask about old scars as if

they aren't what made us the people

we fell in love with.

like the mistakes, the slip-ups, the

coloring outside the lines hadn't made

us the masterpieces we'd become.

luis gabriel

i'd be lying if i said that i didn't enjoy the way you
made me feel so small,
the pre-existing feeling finally having been given an
origin.

was i *feeling* too much?

i wanna sit with you in a parked car,

look into your eyes- count stars,

we could talk about yesterdays

sunset,

laugh off short decades of regrets,

each moment its own,

each word treasured.

luis gabriel

maybe if i hadn't been so sad,

you would have stayed?

was i *feeling* too much?

_____.

it's a game.

and games are meant to be played.

luis gabriel

i cut myself trying to put your pieces together.

was i *feeling* too much?

it makes her sad,

the possibility of meaning nothing to

him one day.

maybe the feelings we can't describe,

are the ones we can call love.

was i *feeling* too much?

we were both a little broken,

that's what made us beautiful.

sometimes he felt like he was trapped

in a shell,

if you saw through it,

you would see his soul.

blue and wavering.

a soft stormy sunset wrapped in skin

and held up by bones.

was i *feeling* too much?

maybe we should kiss a little,

sometimes i miss a little,

when you would hold me,

the warmth of your steady breath against my neck.

he said, "i couldn't have even begun to love you

less, even with each thing i learned."

was i *feeling* too much?

the only thing we owed/owe to each other

was/ is to create something beautiful.

luis gabriel

the things i said out of love?

i meant them.

feeling the warmth of your hand in mine,

i know you'll never find a way to make me regret

them.

was i *feeling* too much?

don't want you to forget it,

just know that i meant it.

when i said you'll always be enough.

i promise to kiss you under the moon,

under its any phase,

under no construct of time, everyday.

i promise to kiss you under the moon,

under any ray-

of silver light or golden sunshine.

i promise to kiss you under the gloom under any

sadness,

bury the madness,

make it mine.

was i *feeling* too much?

i told the stars in the night sky about you.

luis gabriel

we're all listening to the same song,

but thinking about different people.

was i *feeling* too much?

you belong to something beautiful,

something i can't explain.

the things that are meant to be are

the things out of our control.

was i *feeling* too much?

he carries the stars in his eyes.

when it comes to you:

no *what ifs* or *what if we had*

just *what we did* and *what we have.*

was i *feeling* too much?

some called it art,

the art of learning to love beneath the stars.

luis gabriel

you went from being a stranger to someone,

i could watch the stars with.

was i *feeling* too much?

you taught me that it was okay to

stop holding my breath.

to breathe.

luis gabriel

love shouldn't be a losing game.

was i *feeling* too much?

because of you,

i'm finding myself daydreaming

about regular places,

all of their full and empty spaces.

luis gabriel

first loves defined and determined,

rearranged and reworded,

what love was supposed to actually

mean for us.

was i *feeling* too much?

i traded space for flowers,

filled the void between my ribs with

your meteor showers,

the ones you had laced between your lips,

the ones you placed down with a kiss.

luis gabriel

your eyes are a fire i have yet to control.

was i *feeling* too much?

her lips taught him to write poems

about the sky.

luis gabriel

the words he wrote were all for him.

was i *feeling* too much?

at night-

between the empty spaces,

he traces,

his love between her thighs.

in her eyes,

you could catch a glimpse

of the butterflies,

he'd instilled in her chest.

was i *feeling* too much?

his lips were a fire he'd never tasted,

an opportunity he'd always take-

never waste it.

luis gabriel

each touch was like the last,

full of fire but still so soft.

was i *feeling* too much?

maybe it's the things you said in the

dead of night,

that keep my heart at an all-time high.

luis gabriel

his lips were something he could never

forget.

was i *feeling* too much?

he doesn't know it,

but the words i wrote last night?

were written in the moment,

his name always fresh in my mind.

he called it selfish when she worried.

made her feel guilty for trying to protect

the slivers of what she perceived to be love.

was i *feeling* too much?

do you think you could love me?

in the ways i need you too,

not the ways you think you need to?

he asked if i believed in god,

i didn't ,

but i believed in him.

was i *feeling* too much?

you were holding me for just seconds,

but i lived each one like a lifetime.

luis gabriel

he could taste the california sun,

the lingering bitterness reminding him that the

butterflies once stuck in his stomach were gone.

caught, lost, and soured.

under the grey haze of a november morning.

was i *feeling* too much?

everyone knows your name but no one

knows it like i do.

when i saw their two fragile hands holding each
other,

graying and wise,

desperate and shaking,

cautious jealously filled me,

i knew i wanted to know what that was.

what it felt like,

to want to witness the decomposition of life.

to know what it feels like to be a shell of yourself
and still feel complete.

just two casualties of war,

hanging onto each other like brush fire smoke and
blue skies.

was i *feeling* too much?

life would be so beautiful with you.

luis gabriel

you made yourself a ghost when i needed you,

then i believed you,

when you said things were picture perfect,

you were just distracted,

but by the way, you acted,

i knew you being in love, just wasn't the case.

was i *feeling* too much?

you kissed at my imperfections convincing me that

they were just different versions of perfection i

hadn't learned to look at.

luis gabriel

he doesn't know it,

but the words i wrote last night?

were written in the moment,

his name always fresh in my mind.

was i *feeling* too much?

so many memories with his name

attached,

no matter how many times she visits the

same places,

with different faces,

he remains unmatched.

luis gabriel

he was a dream caught in a reality he

had made home.

was i *feeling* too much?

in her eyes,

you could catch a glimpse of the butterflies,

he'd instilled in her chest.

luis gabriel

at night-

between the empty spaces,

he traces,

his love between her thighs.

was i *feeling* too much?

life was just a movie and

he hoped that one day they'd make it

to the end.

luis gabriel

her lips taught him to write poems about the sky.

was i *feeling* too much?

just two souls star gazing,

wondering what the clouds are

pretending to be,

wondering if the future shown in the

stars was for us to see.

luis gabriel

i'd give it all to you.

was i *feeling* too much?

life has us slow dancing in the woods,

thinking things we never thought we

would.

luis gabriel

love,

when we gained it,

everyone blamed it,

for messing us up.

for setting fire to the rules that cut us up,

we would have never made it,

we can thank love,

for making us sick and taking us up.

was i *feeling* too much?

he had decided that she was

something temporary.

he hadn't told her,

she could just read it from the way

his eyes flickered past her into the

void she made out to be everyone

else.

she felt entirely empty.

like

someone

had

drained her

of

her

soul.

was i *feeling* too much?

she was scared of growing invisible,

that one day her smile would look a

little too much like someone else's,

and he'd be gone.

hoping to make them smile.

luis gabriel

you taught me how to love,

and then taught me how it felt to

have it taken-

away.

was i *feeling* too much?

after you,

i realized "i love you" wasn't

something i said when i got scared

and wanted to know that you'd stay.

luis gabriel

his love was light and he had left her in the dark.

was i *feeling* too much?

maybe he had let her know too much

too quickly,

it was like everything he felt for her

and had spoken now meant nothing at all.

he had never pretended with her,

promising things

he knew he could never offer-

not even to himself.

was i *feeling* too much?

it was after

her-

"are we okay?"

when she noticed him grow the most

quiet,

like he was waiting for the silence to speak for him.

and it did.

she already knew what the silence

leaving his lips meant.

he could tell she was overthinking,

diving past the pools of amber brown

in her eyes,

he could see her frantically trying to

piece a puzzle together,

trying to match all her worries to

their solutions

before she breaks.

was i *feeling* too much?

she could see,

that it was in his own body that he

felt the least welcome,

like all the characters he'd written

about were written to be happier than

he had ever hoped he could be.

luis gabriel

she had loved him with everything she

thought was love,

now shes loving with the pieces that

stayed after storm washed away the

weaker and more naive parts of it.

was i *feeling* too much?

i was stuck wondering when i'd stop

being so scared of things repeating

themselves,

like someday you'd wake and decide

that i'm not enough.

that maybe one day i'd wake up and

realize that i was alone in love.

everything inside him had too much

to say,

his bones were screaming for a drop

of sunshine.

was i *feeling* too much?

you're not who you said you were.

luis gabriel

she'd never felt more misunderstood,

it's like they weren't trying to see her

at all.

was i *feeling* too much?

it took you so little

to forget about me at that moment

and fall into someone else.

luis gabriel

i knew it was over when i stopped

liking the parts of me that looked like

you.

"you don't really listen when i talk"

i got used to listening to the empty

promises-

i'd learn to tune him out,

all his carefully crafted cautious words

that were placed on the back shelf of my

mind,

so far back no matter how deeply he

stared-

they'd be too hard to find.

sometimes she wished she could shed her skin,

maybe the feelings in this new skin

would wear leashes,

and the sadness simmering to the top would trickle

out from the soles of her feet,

the sunshine finally feeling warm and and untainted,

yellow sun-

watercolored and softly painted-

hanging above her.

was i *feeling* too much?

you made me realize that not even an infinity

together-

would ever be enough.

she got scared when his "i love yous"

stopped feeling like pinky promises,

the childlike innocence behind them,

always so scared, too careful not to cross

one's fingers,

so she sat there-

hands shaky,

eyes clouded,

lips with words wondering where he'd

been,

her pinky promises,

and their childlike innocence,

growing dim.

was i *feeling* too much?

sleeping alone felt different now. she closed her
eyes and pulled the sheets up higher to cover her
head. it was like all the space between them had laid
itself in the bed.

luis gabriel

you keep saying his name

like it saved you from the dangerous

depths of the water he put you in.

was i *feeling* too much?

if the one that got away came back,

would you still choose me?

luis gabriel

my heart belonged to you,

even before i'd told you that it did.

was i *feeling* too much?

she held herself tighter. pulling and twisting the

loose strands of string at the bottom of her jacket.

she wondered when she'd lose the fear of feeling

lonely. when the loneliness would stop filling the

cavities around her bones.

luis gabriel

i scribbled your face out with a sharpie.

now it's messy, dark, and empty spaces

covering up where your dark eyes,

smile and all the places,

that led the swarming butterflies into my chest.

was i *feeling* too much?

suddenly all of the sad songs,

about all the bad loves,

remind me of you.

luis gabriel

she realized a part of her missed being lonely,

missed when she only felt like all she

needed as herself,

when the stares from far away were

her own reflecting off mirrors

untouched,

when the grazes from fingertips were her own,

soft and hungry-not much.

was i *feeling* too much?

maybe if we had stayed kids,

a time when-

pinky promises weighed more than

they should have,

they could have weighed more than

our empty promises as adults which

should have

meant the world.

what she would do to crawl out of her

skin-

and float into the sky,

to be surrounded by everything while

feeling absolutely nothing at all.

was i *feeling* too much?

i remember feeling sad in january,

they said it'd fade when it became february,

they said the winter had left its mark on me,

i told them no one,

not even my shadow had decided to stay with me.

luis gabriel

we don't get to pretend that nothing

happened.

like we didn't kill something that felt

like it had a life of its own.

was i *feeling* too much?

i was willing to wait until you had learned to love

yourself.

luis gabriel

maybe we're better off as strangers...

maybe it would have killed us to stay

friends after everything we had put each other

through.

was i *feeling* too much?

sometimes she questioned if he knew

what he wanted,

if she could deal with his demons,

if she could deal with the haunted.

the parts of myself that i considered human you

painted out to be flawed.

was i *feeling* too much?

what a torture it was,

feeling like i wasn't enough for either of us.

luis gabriel

he was electricity in her bones.

he had never touched her but somehow he was

always on her skin and at the tips of her finger tips.

was i *feeling* too much?

he's so scared of being alone in love.

she was a puzzle with missing and

broken pieces,

she was just a little damaged,

maybe one day someone would decide

she was worth figuring out,

maybe one day someone would see the bigger

picture,

her soul in its entirety.

was i *feeling* too much?

and maybe when you look at me you

feel nothing at all,

but could you at least pretend?

luis gabriel

we fought last night.....

are you still mad?

did you feel sad?

we didn't make up last night,

thought we were gonna break up last night.

maybe we should have made up last night.

maybe we should've learned to talk

things out instead of fighting last night.

was i *feeling* too much?

maybe she should have stayed invisible.

no one could hurt what they could not see.

i remember the day when i realized i'd never be
enough for you.
i still shudder when i remember how my heart fell
to the bottom of my chest.

she was always reflecting as an outsider,

looking deep into her mind as if she had never

belonged to it,

and the sadness inside her was strange-

a grave of unturned stones.

luis gabriel

memories only remind me

of the empty spaces in-between my fingers,

where yours used to hide-

clenched and sweaty.

was i *feeling* too much?

my words belonged to you,

until you threw them into the fire,

the smell of smoke was stronger than we'd ever

been.

luis gabriel

you photographed strangers,

crooked smiles,

warm eyes,

worn souls,

hoping to preserve their fragile, time-sensitive tales,

while i was fading away in front of you,

hoping you'd notice before the edges of my vision

turned brown and the color grew dim,

before i wrinkled away as the pocket pictures

tucked away in your denim jeans do.

- letters to her lover, the photographer

was i *feeling* too much?

maybe the skies are empty,

and all the warm sunsets are trapped

inside of his chest.

luis gabriel

she realized that feeling "nothing"

would not be feasible,

the numbness where the sadness had

started to bloom would always tug

away at the corners of her mind.

was i *feeling* too much?

when they passed,

they were far gone,

the clouds covering the stars they used to climb up

into the stillness they could call peace.

luis gabriel

she was a window for some,

something to look through and never really

noticed until their fingerprints revealed themselves.

was i *feeling* too much?

there are parts of me that wouldn't forgive the parts

of me that made you fall out of love.

luis gabriel

i'd say i want this forever but i heard that forever

doesn't last as long as heartbreak does.

was i *feeling* too much?

lately, he'd been struggling to create the peace he

wished to feel in the pits of his chest.

luis gabriel

you wondered where the love went when it ran out.

was i *feeling* too much?

maybe the body she felt locked inside of was

perfect,

her skin her own and unique in its entirety.

she felt like the words and emotions

trapped in her chest would push him

away,

like the sadness inside was growing and

growing. the sea of blue pushing past the shore

and crawling onto the deep green.

maybe you and i would remain the same,

nothing changed,

no construct of time redefining us.

was i *feeling* too much?

she just wanted love.

love unexplained, untainted, and

unconditional.

no matter how many letters she sent,

her words never reached LA.

two-thousand carefully crafted love

letters written in quick cursive,

hoping to be read.

understood.

and possibly explored.

two-thousand love letters and her words

never reached LA.

her skin was now a memory,

a friend to his imagination when he found himself

removed from reality,

but even that sometimes felt like it was fading.

head buried into his pillow questioning if that's

what she really felt like,

if that's how she made him feel.

changes, full of maybes and definites.

it'd make me happy to see you happier, maybe

change wouldn't ruin everything, it'd put a bandaid

on a self-defined dull existence for you,

a pivotal upper,

many mornings spent less convinced of self doubt.

maybe change would wiggle it's way into our chests

and we'd start doing other things, seeing each other

less, mentally or physically.

thinking less of each other or thinking more.

changes, full of maybes and definites.

and the inevitable desire for an eternity of standstill.

was i *feeling* too much?

i remember when i ran out of words to share,

i had spent weeks telling myself that i had grown

past the need to feel loved.

luis gabriel

your hands, soiled and unholy,

lips tarnished, red and worn like rusted copper, will

never touch me again.

my daydreams, borrowed sun in a drowning mind-

will never be polluted with 'love explained',

i will never need to know what 'love in action' would feel

like from you,

the old me would say " i would not get to" as if i

would miss out on your shortcomings,

you may have left the inside of my chest war torn,

lungs tired and hungry for something fresh,

heart saddened and gray and blue,

but now they can heal.

and i hope that the best parts of you,

human but wiser,

two parts i did not get to meet, can do that too.

was i *feeling* too much?

sometimes her mind was a train station,

her feelings tiny little people scurrying to different

destinations, some were doing it anxiously, slowly,

and quickly.

all of them leaving the station-rushing to leave her.

leaving behind the thoughts of sadness,

the hundreds of lonely thoughts boarding a train to a

destination unknown and far away from herself.

this body has been changing and i have reluctantly

grown used to the self tailoring and the inevitable

signs of wear.

but-

i say reluctantly because when i look at myself,

all i really see are damaged variations and

fragments of past selves,

all of them silently aching for a drop of the

innocence that they once had when i was wrapped

in fresh skin and untainted eyes.

was i *feeling* too much?

she started wondering if he could love her

ever-changing self,

some days were blue,

some days gray,

some days black,

some days yellow and sunny,

some days rainy and sad.

could he love all of her phases,

all of her,

though small parts of her were in smaller and

different places.

luis gabriel

his voice is medicine for my aching body-

a patchwork of broken wings and soft plumage surrounding

a hummingbird heart overridden by sadness and grief.

was i *feeling* too much?

she remembered letting him stay,

he had stayed until he had killed the happiness she used to

see when she looked at herself in the mirror.

he stayed not because of the love promised but for the love

he had stored away,

for the love he had tucked away for himself in places he

was just starting to see again,

the places where the waves of sadness had finally begun to

run away from shore and empty shallow waters.

was i *feeling* too much?

she looked forward to stop existing in the spaces that no

longer let the sun touch her shadow's horizon.

sometimes he laid in the dark,

head deep in his pillow,

a cloud of thoughts hanging over his head,

the desire for momentary pause struggling to stay afloat

and sometimes drowning.

maybe one day there'd be a stillness,

a little bit of borrowed sunshine.

you said we could have had something beautiful and
broken,

said i ruined it,

that i soiled the way things ended,

but you never took credit for the way you ruined me.

Made in the USA
Las Vegas, NV
30 November 2024